Science Biographies

Thomas
Edison

Kay Barnham

Raintree
Chicago, Illinois

© 2014 Raintree
an imprint of Capstone Global Library, LLC
Chicago, Illinois

To contact Capstone Global Library please call
800-747-4992, or visit our web site www.capstonepub.com

Edited by Dan Nunn, Adam Miller, and Diyan Leake
Designed by Cynthia Akiyoshi
Picture research by Tracy Cummins
Production by Helen McCreath
Originated by Capstone Global Library
Printed and bound in China

17 16 15 14 13
10 9 8 7 6 5 4 3 2 1

Library of Congress Cataloging-in-Publication Data
Barnham, Kay. author.
  Thomas Edison / Kay Barnham.
    pages cm.—(Science biographies)
  Summary: "This book traces the life of Thomas Edison,
from his early childhood and education through his sources
of inspiration and challenges faced, early successes, and the
many inventions for which he is best known. A timeline
at the end of the book summarizes key milestones and
achievements of Edison's life."—Provided by publisher.
  Includes bibliographical references and index.
  ISBN 978-1-4109-6239-3 (hb)—ISBN 978-1-4109-6246-1 (pb)
1. Edison, Thomas A. (Thomas Alva), 1847-1931—Juvenile
literature. 2. Inventors—United States—Biography—
Juvenile literature. 3. Electrical engineers—United States—
Biography—Juvenile literature. 4. Menlo Park (N.J.)—
History—Juvenile literature. I. Title.
  TK140.E3B336 2014
  621.3092—dc23   2013014220

Acknowledgments
We would like to thank the following for permission to
reproduce photographs: Alamy p. 21 (© RGB Ventures
LLC dba SuperStock); Corbis pp. 6 (Bettmann), 17 (Library
of Congress via Science Faction), 18 (Bettmann); Getty
Images pp. 5 (Archive Photos), 7 (Time & Life Pictures),
9 (Keystone-France), 11 (David E. Scherman/Time Life
Pictures), 13 (Prisma/UIG), 25 (Hulton Archive), 26
(Science Faction/Library of Congress), 28 (Roger Viollet);
From the collections of The Henry Ford p. 27 (THF37936);
istockphoto design elements (© James Steidl); Library of
Congress Prints and Photographs Division pp. 4, 16, 22,
23; National Archives design elements; NPS Photo p. 12;
Science Photo Library p. 10; Shutterstock p. 8 (© Anneka),
design elements (© Antonio Abrignani, © Morphart
Creation, © Terence Mendoza, © FotoSergio, © Kellis,
© Inga Nielsen, © lynea, © Ratana21); Superstock pp. 15
(Dennis MacDonald), 19 bottom (Science Museum/SSPL),
20 (Everett Collection), 24 (Science and Society); Topfoto
p. 14 (Topham Picturepoint).

Cover photographs reproduced with permission of
Superstock (Stock Montage) and Photo Researchers, Inc.
(John M. Daugherty).

Every effort has been made to contact copyright holders of
material reproduced in this book. Any omissions will
be rectified in subsequent printings if notice is given to
the publisher.

All the Internet addresses (URLs) given in this book were
valid at the time of going to press. However, due to the
dynamic nature of the Internet, some addresses may have
changed, or sites may have changed or ceased to exist since
publication. While the author and publisher regret any
inconvenience this may cause readers, no responsibility for
any such changes can be accepted by either the author or
the publisher.

Contents

Who Was Thomas Edison?   4

Young Edison   6

Edison the Telegraph Operator   8

Edison the Businessman   10

Edison's Family   12

The Wizard of Menlo Park   14

The Phonograph   16

The Light Bulb   18

Light for Everyone!   20

New Beginnings   22

Motion Pictures   24

Into the 20th Century   26

After Edison   28

Timeline   *29*

Glossary   *30*

Find Out More   *31*

Index   *32*

Some words are shown in **bold**, like this. You can find out what they mean by looking in the glossary.

Who Was Thomas Edison?

Thomas Edison (1847–1931) was an American inventor. His most famous inventions were the electric light bulb, the **phonograph**, and the **motion picture** camera.

Edison wasn't just an inventor. He was also a businessman. He wanted to invent things that people would buy, so that he would make money. If Edison saw a good idea, he would work hard to make it even better.

Edison famously said that genius is "one percent inspiration, ninety-nine percent perspiration."

The United States in Edison's day

The 19th century was a time of great change in the United States. Millions of people were moving there from other countries to start a new life. New **industries** were appearing in the northeast, while railroads were being built across the country. This meant that people could travel west, too.

Edison's first job was on the railroads. In this picture, railroad workers are joining the Central Pacific Railroad and the Union Pacific Railroad at Promontory Summit, Utah, in 1869.

Young Edison

Thomas Alva Edison was born on February 11, 1847, in Milan, Ohio. Al—as his family nicknamed him—was the youngest of seven children.

When Thomas was about eight, he went to school. His teacher could not keep up with his questions, so he left after just three months. From then on, Thomas's mother taught him at home. He was always very grateful to his mother for spending so much time teaching him. He wanted to make her proud.

Thomas's favorite subject was science. He loved it so much that he built a **laboratory** for his own experiments.

Thomas was a lively, curious boy who asked lots of questions about how things worked.

EARNING MONEY

Thomas was eager to start earning money, and by the age of 12 he had a job. He sold snacks, candy, and newspapers on the Grand Trunk railroad line. Soon, he was printing his own weekly newspaper—the *Grand Trunk Herald*—and selling that, too.

Steam locomotives carried passengers along the Grand Trunk Railroad in Canada and the United States. Thomas worked on the trains that ran between Port Huron and Detroit, in Michigan.

Edison the Telegraph Operator

In 1862, Thomas saved the life of a little boy who had strayed onto a railroad track—and his own life changed forever. The boy's father was a **telegraph** operator. He was so grateful to Thomas that he taught him how to use a telegraph machine. Now, Thomas could get a job as a telegraph operator!

Telegraphy

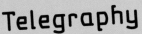

By the 1860s, telegraphy had become the fastest way of sending messages around the world. Telegraph machines, like this one designed by Samuel Morse, sent messages along a wire using electrical signals. The first long-distance telephone call did not happen until 1915.

Edison traveled around the United States for years working as a telegraph operator. But he was **ambitious**. He spent his spare time experimenting with new ideas. He loved inventing and hoped that one of his inventions would make his fortune.

Edison sometimes worked night shifts. When he wasn't busy, he could perform experiments.

Edison the Businessman

In 1869, Edison **patented** his first invention: the electric vote recorder. This machine was designed to save time during elections. Instead of people counting the votes by hand, the machine would do all the hard work. But sales were poor, and Edison was disappointed. He decided that from now he would not "waste time inventing things that people would not want to buy."

What is a patent?

A patent is a **license** the government gives. It is proof that a person came up with an idea or invention. Other people are not allowed to copy the idea, unless they pay a fee to the person who holds the patent.

Edison's vote recorder meant that voters did not have to fill out ballots—they simply moved a switch on the **device**.

SUCCESS!

In 1869, Edison left his job and moved to New York City. Here, at last, he started to have some success with his ideas.

Edison invented a new type of **stock ticker** that printed messages in letters and numbers instead of **Morse code**. It meant that traders in **stocks** could get information about prices faster and then make more money.

Thousands of stock tickers were sold. They were used well into the 20th century.

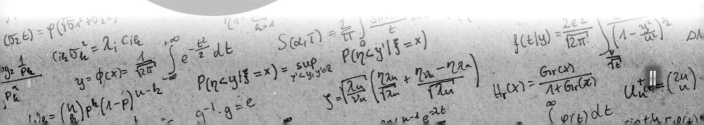

Edison's Family

The money Edison made from his stock ticker was enough to open his own business. His employees made and sold telegraph equipment, and there was room for Edison to invent, too.

DOT AND DASH

Mary Stilwell was a worker in Edison's telegraph company. Just two months after she and Edison met, they got married. They had three children together. The first two children were named Marion and Thomas, but Edison nicknamed them "Dot" and "Dash," after the short and long signals used in Morse code.

Mary Stilwell married Thomas Edison on Christmas Day 1871. She was 16 years old. He was 24.

MORE SUCCESS!

Edison continued inventing. One of his biggest successes was the quadruplex telegraph machine. It could send not just one but *four* messages at the same time!

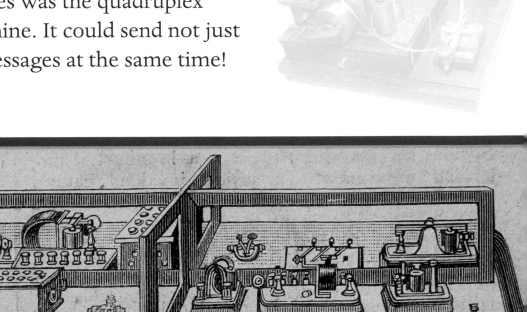

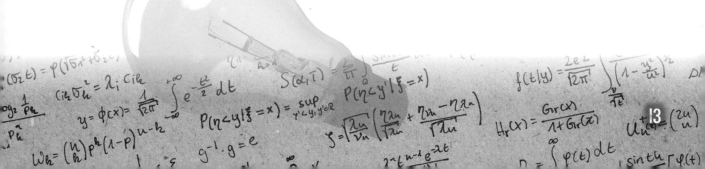

The quadruplex telegraph transmitter saved telegraph companies a lot of money—and made Edison a lot of money, too.

The quadruplex telegraph transmitter sent two messages in one direction at the some time that another two messages were being sent in the opposite direction.

The Wizard of Menlo Park

Soon, Edison had a problem. He wanted to employ more people to help him work on his many ideas and inventions, but there just was not enough space for them in his workshop. He needed more room.

In 1876, the Edison family moved to Menlo Park, New Jersey, where Edison built a research laboratory. He invented so many amazing things here that he became known as the Wizard of Menlo Park.

Edison's research laboratory at Menlo Park was the first of its kind.

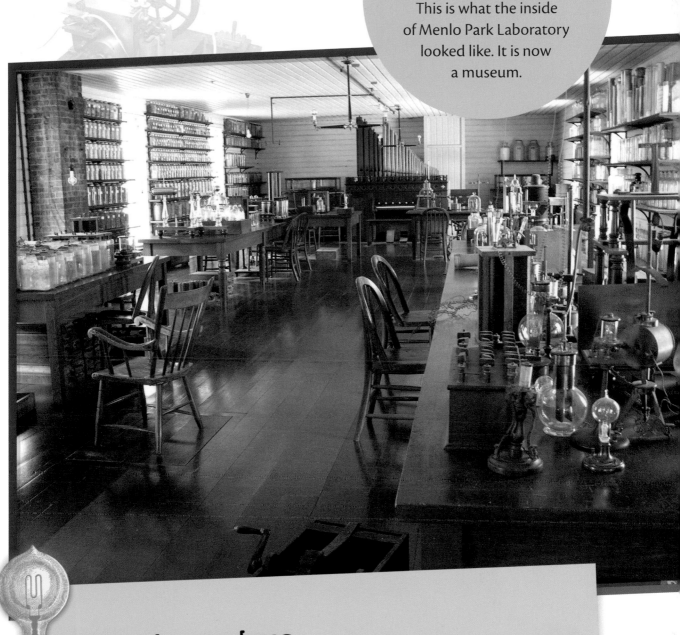

This is what the inside of Menlo Park Laboratory looked like. It is now a museum.

Edison's muckers

Thomas Edison called his laboratory workers "muckers," while he was the "chief mucker." First, Edison had an idea for a device or thought of a way to make something work better. Then, a team of muckers would make and test the idea. Different teams worked on different ideas at the same time, so Edison could invent and patent many ideas at once.

The Phonograph

Edison invented the phonograph at Menlo Park. Other inventors had already made machines that recorded sound, but Edison's phonograph did something totally new— it played recorded sound back, too.

As soon as the phonograph was built, Edison recorded his own voice. He said the nursery rhyme "Mary had a little lamb," and he was delighted when the phonograph played it right back to him.

This shows Thomas Edison and his second version of the phonograph. He came up with the idea while he was trying to find a way to record telephone messages.

This invention by Edison recorded sound on wax cylinders.

Why were phonographs important?

Phonographs were the first way of recording and playing back sound. Edison's early recordings were made on tinfoil sheets, but later they were made on wax cylinders. The next important invention was the gramophone, which played flat, circular, **vinyl** records. Today, music is often recorded **digitally**, but many people still prefer to play vinyl records.

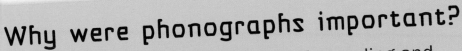

The Light Bulb

Edison's next great idea was the one for which he is most remembered: the light bulb.

The British scientist Joseph Swan invented the first light bulb to use a carbon filament— a fine thread that glowed when electricity traveled through it. There was a **vacuum** inside the bulb, which meant there was no oxygen inside it. Without oxygen, Swan's light bulb stayed lit. However, the light would only last 13 hours.

Joseph Swan demonstrated his light bulb in 1878, but it did not glow for very long.

Swan wrote about his ideas in a science magazine so that everyone could read about it. The very next year, Edison patented his own light bulb. It was very similar to Swan's invention.

Edison tried to improve his light bulb. By 1880, it glowed for over 1,200 hours.

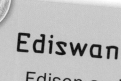

Ediswan

Edison and Swan argued over who had invented the light bulb. Finally, in 1883, they formed a company called Ediswan and agreed to work together.

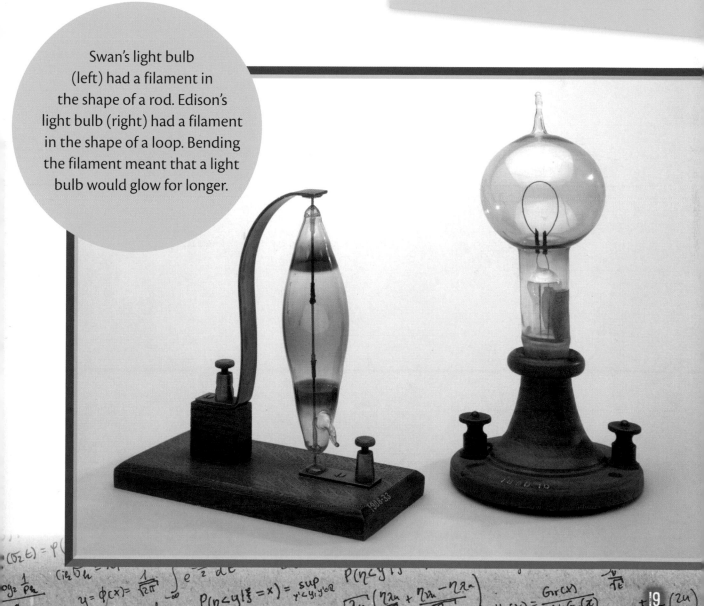

Swan's light bulb (left) had a filament in the shape of a rod. Edison's light bulb (right) had a filament in the shape of a loop. Bending the filament meant that a light bulb would glow for longer.

Light for Everyone!

Edison worked on making light bulbs that glowed for many hours. He also tried to make them much cheaper, so that everyone could buy them. However, light bulbs need electricity to make them work. So the next thing Edison did was to develop a way to supply electricity to customers, too. In 1882, he opened a power station on Pearl Street in New York City—the first of its kind.

When it opened in 1882, Pearl Street power station generated electricity for just a few hundred light bulbs. Fifty-two of these light bulbs lit the offices of the *New York Times* newspaper, which was a few streets away.

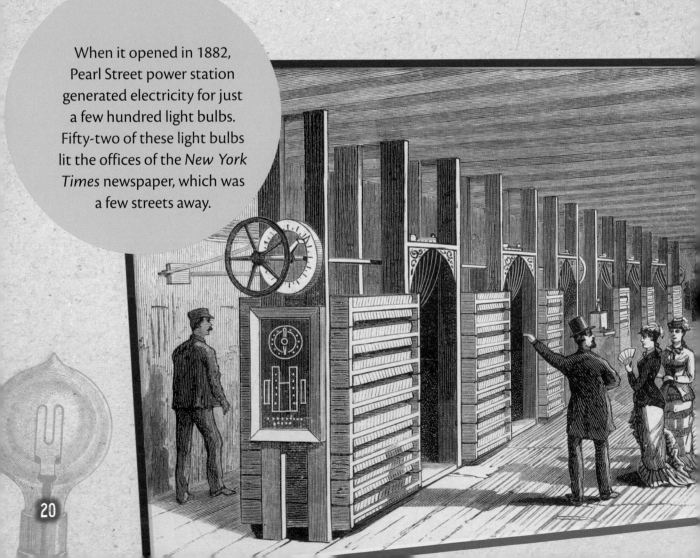

AC versus DC

When electricity was first generated, there were different ways of supplying it to customers. The inventor Nikola Tesla was a big fan of the **alternating current (AC)** system. Meanwhile, Edison thought that **direct current (DC)** was the future. This time Edison was wrong. The AC system is still used today.

Nikola Tesla was a Serbian inventor who had once worked for Edison.

New Beginnings

In 1884, Edison's wife, Mary, died. She was just 29. Edison had already been spending a lot of time away from Menlo Park, working in New York City. Now he moved his children there, too. It was a sad time for all of them.

A year later, Edison and his family visited friends in New England. It was here that he met Mina Miller, the daughter of another inventor.
In 1886, they were married. The family moved to West Orange, New Jersey.

Mina Miller was 20 when she married Edison. He was 39.

Edison's new laboratory in West Orange was built in 1887. It was much bigger than his laboratory at Menlo Park. Half of Edison's inventions would be developed here.

When Edison's West Orange Laboratory opened, he employed about 200 people there.

Motion Pictures

In 1894, Edison's team invented a very early motion-picture machine called the Kinetoscope. Edison did not think there was much of a future for motion pictures and he did not file international patents. This meant that inventors overseas could copy and improve his ideas. That is exactly what they did. In France, the Lumière brothers patented the hugely successful cinématographe in 1895. They recorded and showed films to large audiences.

The Kinetoscope had a major drawback. It could be used by just one person at a time.

Edison did not want to be outdone. He soon became involved with another **projector** called the Vitascope. Edison even built his own film studio at West Orange, to make motion pictures for the new projector.

In this publicity shot, Thomas Edison is shown holding a piece of film.

Into the 20th Century

One of Edison's final successes was the nickel-iron battery, which was manufactured from 1903 to 1975.

During World War I (1914–1918), Edison became head of the Naval Consulting Board. This was a group of scientists and inventors who worked together to research and develop ideas that would help the United States in wartime.

Edison was a friend of the car manufacturer Henry Ford. In 1929—the 50th anniversary of Edison's electric light bulb—Ford transported Edison's Menlo Park laboratory all the way to Dearborn, Michigan. He opened it as a museum.

Edison died two years later.

Edison's nickel-iron battery was used to power electric vehicles, like this one in 1910. The battery was rechargeable. Today, scientists are trying to improve Edison's battery so that it can be used in modern cars.

To celebrate the **golden jubilee** of the invention of Edison's light bulb, Henry Ford held a huge dinner in his honor. The guests included Marie Curie, Orville Wright, and President Herbert Hoover.

After Edison

Thomas Alva Edison patented an astonishing 1,093 different inventions during his lifetime. Without him, communication, electric lighting, electricity supplies, sound recording, movies, and many other advances in technology might have been very, very different. Edison's ideas changed millions of people's lives.

This photo shows Edison with the light bulbs he invented. In 1929, many cities and buildings across the United States, such as the Boston Public Library, were lit up to celebrate the golden jubilee of the light bulb.

Timeline

1847 Thomas Alva Edison is born in Milan, Ohio, on February 11

1859 Begins his first job on the railroads

1863 Starts working as a telegraph operator

1869 Registers his first patent, for the electric vote recorder; becomes a full-time inventor and moves to New York City; makes improvements to the stock ticker

1871 Marries Mary Stilwell

1874 Invents the quadruplex telegraph

1876 Moves to Menlo Park, New Jersey

1877 Invents the phonograph

1879 Registers his first light bulb patent

1882 Opens the Pearl Street power station

1884 Mary Stilwell dies

1886 Edison marries Mina Miller

1887 Moves to West Orange, New Jersey

1900 Begins work on the nickel-iron rechargeable battery

1929 Celebrates the light bulb's golden jubilee with Henry Ford

1931 Thomas Edison dies on October 18, at age 84

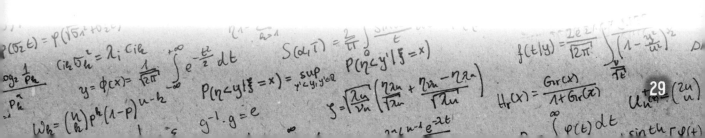

Glossary

alternating current (AC) way of supplying electricity in which the electric current changes direction many times every second

ambitious wants to do well in life and work

device something made to do a particular job

digitally way of storing information as numbers so that it can be understood by a computer or other electronic device

direct current (DC) way of supplying electricity in which the electric current travels in just one direction

golden jubilee celebration on the 50th anniversary of an event

industry type of business that has to do with making something

laboratory place where science experiments and research are carried out

license permission to own, use, or do something

Morse code alphabet in which each letter is expressed as a different combination of dots and dashes. For example, the letter A is . – and the letter B is – ... . These dots and dashes can be sent as signals along a telegraph wire.

motion picture old-fashioned name for a movie

patent have a license that shows that someone has invented something and nobody else can make it without paying the inventor a fee

phonograph very early machine that played sound and music

projector machine used to show film on a big screen

stock ticker machine that prints the prices of stocks onto a paper strip called ticker tape

stocks small parts of a company or business that are owned by different people. Stocks, sometimes also called shares, are bought and sold in a stock exchange.

telegraph system for sending messages along a wire as a series of electrical signals

vacuum space that has had all the air—including gases such as oxygen—removed

vinyl type of plastic used to make records

Find Out More

BOOKS

Adkins, Jan. *Thomas Edison* (DK Biography). New York: Dorling
Kindersley, 2009.

Garcia, Tracy J. *Thomas Edison* (Junior Graphic American Inventors).
New York: PowerKids, 2013.

INTERNET SITES

Facthound offers a safe, fun way to find Internet sites related to this book. All of
the sites on Facthound have been researched by our staff.

Here's all you do:

Visit **www.facthound.com**

Type in this code: 9781410962393

PLACES TO VISIT

Edison Birthplacc Museum

9 Edison Drive

Milan, Ohio 44846

www.tomedison.org

Edison and Ford Winter Estates

2350 McGregor Boulevard

Fort Myers, Florida 33901

www.edisonfordwinterestates.org

The Thomas Edison Center at Menlo Park

37 Christie Street

Edison, New Jersey 08820

www.menloparkmuseum.org

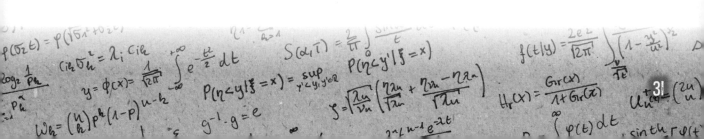

Index

alternating current (AC) 21

batteries 26, 27

carbon filaments 18, 19
cinématographe 24
Curie, Marie 27

death of Edison 26
digital music 17
direct current (DC) 21

Edison, Mary 12
Edison, Mina 22
Ediswan 19
electric vehicles 27
electric vote recorders 10
electricity 20–21
experiments 6, 9

Ford, Henry 26, 27

genius 4
gramophones 17

Hoover, Herbert 27

Kinetoscope 24

laboratories 6, 14, 15, 23, 26
light bulbs 18–19, 20, 27, 28
Lumière brothers 24

marriage and children 12, 22
Menlo Park 14, 15, 16, 26
Morse, Samuel 8
Morse code 8, 11, 12
motion pictures 24–25
muckers 15

Naval Consulting Board 26

patents 10, 15, 24, 28
phonographs 16–17
power stations 20

quadruplex telegraph machines 13

railroads 5, 7

sound recording 16, 17
steam locomotives 7
stock tickers 11
stocks 11
Swan, Joseph 18–19

telegraphy 8, 9, 12, 13
Tesla, Nikola 21

vinyl records 17
Vitascope 25

wax cylinder recordings 17
West Orange Laboratory 22, 23, 25
World War I 26
Wright, Orville 27